90% OFF —Every Day!

Diana Tenes

For additional copies of this book,
shopping tour info,
Speaking Requests,
or for more information,
Please contact Diana Tenes through her Web site:
www.IMakeFaces.com

The Kindle edition of "90% Off Every Day!" is available.

Cover and title page illustrations by
caricature artist Mark Z-Man.
www.flash.net/~zmanart

Why I Wrote This Book

I have to look good and have a wide variety of clothes and costumes for all of the jobs I do.

I'm a make-up artist, actress, model, and face painter. I'm also a single mom with a son.

I often get complimented on my wardrobe. People often ask, where did you get that?

When I say "at a thrift store," (which is where I purchase the majority of my clothing most of the time), people are often shocked, surprised, or think I'm joking.

The first question people ask me is, what thrift stores do you go to? Like if I tell them where I shop I am giving the best secret away. I say it doesn't matter what thrift store you go to. This is the answer to that question.

There's good stuff there, you just have to find it. It is like a treasure hunt. It is a hunt, a skill, to shop well, no matter where you are shopping. Whether you are shopping at Neiman Marcus, the supermarket, or the thrift store. Of course there's junk, or ill made goods as anywhere you go to shop. You learn to eliminate the junk and get what works for you.

This is what this book is about. It is mostly about shopping thrift stores. But it is also about respecting other peoples products, conserving our planet through recycling and having fun and saving money all at the same time.

Contents

Treasure Hunt Stories

This story is about a favorite dress that I have had for about twenty years. I was driving down the street and I noticed a thrift store that I had never seen before. There were a couple of other thrift stores on the block. I almost walked right by this one, because it looked so disheveled. The door was open and things were just sitting in and on cardboard boxes along the walls. There was a display case and a man with cash register behind it. It looked as if it was an abandoned store going out of business.

I didn't find anything. As I walked out, there was an old rack with a few items of clothing hung on some twisted wire hangers. I went through them, quickly touching them with my hand. I stopped when I touched fabric that I had never felt before. I pulled the garment off the hanger and held it up to see what it was. It was a hand-knitted vintage dress, from the 30s, in turquoise, cream, black, and gray rayon yarns. It had hand-made glazed floral buttons on it. I have never seen anything like it, ever. It was gorgeous. I looked at the sign on the rack, and it said 50 cents. I ran into the store and threw the dress on the counter. I told the man it was 50 cents, as I scrambled to get change out of my purse, I got out of breath. I got it. I bought it—it was mine. A treasure to keep, to hold, and to love, and wear for many years to come. This was not an average dress.

What Is in My Closet?

If you came to my home and looked in my closet, you would find that 95% of my clothes, shoes, and accessories are from thrift stores. All I have is great high quality clothing. Every time my friends or sisters see me, their comments are along these lines: "You didn't get that at the THRIFT STORE did you?"!

People always ask me: "What thrift store do you go to?" I tell them it doesn't make any difference what thrift store you go to. You just go and look for what you want. There are great things everywhere, but you have to have an open mind to finding other terrific finds.

Now I'm going to my closet to tell you exactly what I have bought in various thrift stores in my neighborhood; by style, fabric, brand, and price.

These are the clothes I wear to work as a makeup artist in department stores such as Saks Fifth Avenue, Macy's, Neiman Marcus and Nordstrom.

- Givenchy, boutique skirt, fine wool made in France, size 36, cost– $8.00.

- Silk designer-lined skirt, ruffled hem, size 6, cost–$3.00.

- Esprit drawstring acetate/rayon satin skirt, size 7/8, cost–$10.00.

- Andrea Jove's wool knit, knee length, straight skirt, cost–$4.00
- Guess Collection nylon/spandex trouser skirt, size 2, cost–$5.00
- Wool/acetate skirt with a metallic ribbon laced hem, made in Italy, size M, cost–$3.00
- Tahari, black rayon lace, fitted knee length, lined skirt, cost–$4.00
- Nordstrom, size S. Petite Premiere Collections, 100% knit, Merino wool skirt, cost–$6.00
- Sheer silk Kimono blouse with silk, satin trim, 1 size, cost–$3.00
- Sheer mesh, long-sleeve T -shirt w/blue metallic butterflies, ruffled edges, cost–$2.00
- Silk, satin Black Chinese brocade vest with frog buttons, cost–$4.00
- Silk/ cotton knit, sleeveless shell, size small, cost–$8.00
- Rampage, a short sleeve turtleneck made with spandex nylon, size S, cost–$2.50
- Macy's Charter Club Petite wool ribbed sweater with tie in a size S, cost–$5.00
- Donatella, made in France, size 38 long sleeve turtle nylon, cost–$5.00.
- Vintage 50s wool sleeves shell with black trim and rhinestones, no size, cost–$5.00

- Nordstroms Intimate long sleeve, nylon body suit, in a size S, cost–$6.00

- Wilkes Sport—Wilkes Bashford, wool double-knit long sleeve sweater with zipper neck, size 2, cost–$4.00.

- Erik Stewart cotton/silk crew neck sweater, size S, cost–$4.00

- Jay Jacks silk open collar, long sleeve blouse, cost–$5.00

- Alaia Paris rayon knit sweater coat, no size, cost–$6.00

- Anne Klein acetate rayon blazer, size 2, cost–$3.00

- BEBE (size 2), rayon jacket, fitted, cost–$4.00

- Preview collection (2), wool jacket, cost–$3.50.

- Betsy Johnson, velvet, black ,rhinestone button, sweater coat with buttons, cost–$6.50

- J. Crew black cotton velvet jeans (size 2), cost–$6.50

- J. Crew black satin slacks (2), cost–$8.00.

- Banana Republic silk lined slacks, size 4, cost–$2.00

I have bought the majority of these items the last six months. I am a motivated, a single mom, an actress and make-up artist with a teenage boy. I have to look good for my work. I wouldn't even touch these items at a 50% off rack in a department store. I could, but I would have to save and I would be just as picky and selective. Shopping at the thrift store is relaxing and fun. I can spend 5 minutes or 50 minutes in a thrift store and it doesn't matter. Sometimes I find stuff immediately and sometimes not till I am ready to walk out the front door.

Thrift Store Shopping: The Absolute Best Value for My Time and Energy

The energy I put into thrift store shopping gives me higher returns for my dollars and time. No credit card bills. Most thrift stores have sale days, senior discounts, $1.00 racks and even free merchandise with a coupon card. Some even take returns, as long as you have the receipt. It's easier to return something at a thrift store than it is at a regular store. You can always find a manager or employee who will help you.

I've been a clothing designer, costume designer, clothing sales person, wardrobe stylist. I model, act, and am a make-up artist. I've had the opportunity to learn and know a tremendous amount about clothes. But I am also a single mom and it has been practical for me to regularly shop at thrift stores.

All I have to do is go to the department store and look for a pair of pants for myself. I get so disgusted and appalled by the prices that I run back to the thrift store. I find a basic pair of pants on sale for $29.00 to $39.00, and their regular price is $50.00 or $60.00. These pants are okay, but not outstanding. I can go to the thrift store and find an okay pair of pants for $3.00 or $4.00 and find an outstanding pair for $5.00 or $6.00.

Thrift store shopping is great for getting the absolute best value for your time and money. It is also a way of appreciating other people's stuff.

Why do I love thrift stores? I feel so good when I buy something for a fraction of the price of what it's worth. It's a gift that I can appreciate.

Value is not just how much you pay for something—it is in the inherent worth of that object to you. The value is whether or not it serves its purpose in your life. I could own a gorgeous cashmere coat, but if I never wear it, is it of value to me, or just taking up room in my closet?

If it makes me feel good just to know that I own it, and I enjoy owning it, then it's worth keeping.

That's what artwork is in life. It decorates the wall, the room, and hopefully gives you inspiration and good feeling and cheer.

I can go into any thrift store and find something of value. But I'm not necessarily going to buy it just because I like it, or it's cheap. As with anywhere else I chose to shop, I determine it's value for me.

Why Shop at a Retail Store?

Namely for the latest trends. You'll pay top price for the most current styles of clothing. You will look like everybody else and *pay more for it.*

Quality merchandise. You don't want to wear used clothes. You know you can predict that something will be there. *Not always true.*

You are willing to pay top price, to get what you want when you want it. You want to only wear new clothes. You don't have time to shop thrift stores. You don't have enough patience.

Why Shop at a Thrift Store?

It's fun. It is entertaining. You save 75–99% of the original retail cost of anything you buy. You can often find, and regularly purchase new items at thrift stores. You get original clothing that no one else has. You can buy designer clothes for a fraction of the normal price.

There is such a wide variety of clothing, sizes, diversity of various objects. Where can you go and find new things, collectibles, things from almost every era, 20's to 90's and from all over the world all in one store? It is an educational and entertaining experience. You never know what you are going to find.

Who Shops at a Thrift Store?

Not who you might expect.

You may have already shopped at a thrift store and never thought about it. Halloween is a favorite time for people to come by and get a costume from favorite finds. People are often amazed at the quality of their costume finds, but don't consider shopping there for other things. Consider it a learning opportunity for your wallet.

People on a budget who have just moved and needing to get a home started right away stop by and stock up on basic essentials.

Collectors of all types shop at thrift stores for their favorite hard to find items. They know people often throw out good stuff, not realizing it's value or worth. Things that are useless to someone but are a collectors dream. Some collectors shop, just to resell things on EBay, in their antique, collectible or consignment stores.

One secret of stylists for photographers/films, interior decorators, art directors, costume and fashion designers, is shopping at thrift stores. They shop second-hand for inspiration and for lovely things,such as vintage handbags, jewelry, evening gowns, furniture, accessories, toys, household items, dinnerware and silverware, etc.

I like shopping at thrift stores, rather than flea markets, swap meets, garage sales, rummage sales, or even regular retail or outlets. etc. Some people will give to their favorite charity that has a thrift store.

My favorite place to shop is a thrift store. Garage sales are limited to one person's stuff, which doesn't offer much in the way of selection. The best garage sales are block sales, which are multi-famillies, or whole house estates, or moving sales. These types provide more varied stuff to choose from. Garage sales are a good place to buy furniture because many people do not like to move their furniture. They would rather have someone buy and haul it away. You are apt to get a good price, unless it is very expensive, and they are trying to get money out of it.

I appreciate fine quality things, and I have the means to buy whatever I like at a thrift store. Some people feel that way about garage sales. I personally don't like someone staring at me going through their things, and asking for (sometimes) ridiculous amounts of money. You *can* get a good buy, but you need to get to garage sales early. Anything they don't sell usually goes to a thrift store. I find that people who do not want to hassle with a garage sale often give their great stuff to thrift stores.

And thrift stores are open seven days a week depending on where you live and who is operating them.

My First Time in a Thrift Store

I went to a thrift store for the first time when I was 14. I wasn't sure what to expect. Was it stuff from dead people? Where *does* it come from? The thrift store was a huge warehouse with cement floors and with racks and racks of clothes neatly lined up, dishes, furniture, toys, refrigerators, washers, and TVs. It looked like a regular department store with bright lights, even shopping carts, cash registers, and sales signs.

I went with my aunt. She took the whole family as an excursion and we walked around gingerly, up and down the aisles, staring in amazement.

We were all just looking, not touching, just looking. Finally, my mom and aunt started to touch the clothes, really starting to shop. I thought maybe I can find something, too. I made my first purchase and still have it today. It was a tiny brass pill box with crystal rhinestones on top. It cost 25 cents, about 90% less than you could get it for in any other store. I don't know why I have kept it for so long. This box still holds the magic of discovery for me, and introduced me to buying lovely things for the fraction of the price.

I could afford to shop at the thrift store. The one place I could go to as a teen and afford things. I loved clothes then and still do. I remember I bought a purple wool skirt. It was one of my favorite items of clothing in high school. I bought beaded sweaters from the 50s, which are now worth a small fortune, in good condition. I collect clothes like people collect dishes, cards, rocks, cars, or stamps. I trade them in, stare at them, and play with them. It's a professional hobby. I enjoy it very much.

I've Been to Thrift Stores and All I Ever Find Is Junk!

Nonprofit organizations run most thrift stores. Most of the nonprofits are run by dedicated volunteers who want to help their favorite organization earn money. They can be among the most discriminating, well-run shops around. Some are for profit. Like any business, it runs as well as the management, employees, and its organizational skills.

Some thrift stores are set up exactly like a department store, with furniture and appliance sections, areas for women, children, mens and even designer boutiques within the store. Others are small, cute, little boutiques with more specialized items, like clothing and household items.

Thrift stores would not be in business nor consignment or flea markets if what was selling was not saleable. That is why thrift stores often have new merchandise.

What do you think happens to all of that clearance/sale merchandise from department stores or specialty shops that have gone out of business? A store or business can get a tax writeoff when donating new merchandise (or any merchandise) to a thrift store, just like an individual or a family can.

They can only keep it for a certain period of time and they have to get rid of it. Some of it will go to consignment stores, outlets or flea market establishments, etc.

New Clothes at a Thrift Store? Where Do They Come From?

Divorce. Marriage.
Lose weight or gain weight.
Moving. Changing careers, lifestyles, or hobbies.
Cleaning out the closet.
Stores going out of business.
Mark downs.
Clearance.
Unopened gifts.
Living together.
Did not want to exchange it.
Put on a shelf.
Saved for the right day.
Changed your mind.
Cleaners; people forget to pick up their clothes.
Alterations.
Lost articles clothing.
No room for stuff.
Tired of renting storage space.
Out of style.
Needs repair.
Don't Have a receipt

Why Do You Give Clothes Away?

Because they don't fit, too big, too small, too any-
thing!
Don't like them . . .
Out of style.
Worn out.
Need repair.
Don't wear it.
Does not go with anything else!
Doesn't fit into current lifestyle.
Need to clear out of the closet.
Purchased something, and didn't bother to
    exchange it.

Why I Get Rid of Clothes

I like them but I don't wear them.
I have something similar that I wear.
I don't like it anymore.
It's too big or small.
It never fit right.
It is uncomfortable.
It needs to be repaired.
It doesn't go with anything else.
I have nowhere to wear it.

I am tired of looking at it.
It reminds me of a negative person, or situation.

More Reasons Why I Get Rid of Clothes

It takes up precious closet or drawer space.
Someone else can use them.
Might make some extra cash.
You could make someone else happy.
You will feel good to get rid of the stuff you are
    not using.
It makes it easier to get dressed in the morning,
    with fewer choices, less laundry and dry
    cleaning.
You can afford the best.

What Clothing Brands Can I Find Regularly in a Thrift Store?

You can find almost any brand that you can find
in your favorite store, be it a department store or

specialty shop. You can find brands from Nordstrom, Macy's, Mervyn's, Neiman Marcus, Bloomingdales, Penneys, Mervyn's, Walmart, KMart, Sears, etc.

Specific brands that I find regularly include: GAP, Banana Republic, Old Navy, Ann Taylor, Liz Claiborne, Esprit, Levi, Dockers, Talbots, Anchor Blue, Pendleton, Lands End, OshKosh, Anne Klein, and Byer.

I occasionally find American and European designer labels and higher-quality labels such as: Gaultier, Escada, Givenchy, YSL, Betsey Johnson, J. Crew, LL Bean, Vicky Tiel, Jessica McClintock, Scott Mc Clintock.

Best Things to Find at a Thrift Store

special sizes
large
maternity
small women's clothing from 0–6
kids clothes
mens suits
women's suits, dresses, and formals
jeans
purses

coats
paperback books
t-shirts
baseball caps

Kids' clothes are great bargains, up to about ages 5 to 6. After this age they wear them out. You can purchase them for 25 to 50 cents per item. Fifty cents and $1.00 are great prices for kids' clothes. Older children's clothes are much harder to find, unless they wear adult sizes. But, you can find dresses, boots, and shoes for girls. Consignment stores are better for school age clothes.

Men's clothes, You'll find dozens of sport coats, suits, shirts, jackets, blazers, jeans, slacks, belts, and shoes

Evening attire can be the most expensive and wasteful of any occasion. From proms, weddings, reunions, cocktail parties, dances, graduations to formal dinners. People dress down a lot more, but proms and weddings are still formal. Thrift stores are a great place to find evening gowns, little bags and evening sandals. Most have been worn only once.

Consignment shops also carry these items. You can get luxurious gowns for a fraction of the price. I recommend separates for most dressier occasions. I look for sparkly, beaded, sequin tops, silk blouses, and skirts.

I have also found women's and junior's clothing in the kid's department. If you wear smaller sizes, like XS, S, or petites 0 to 5, they sometimes get mixed in with the kid's clothing. I found a Laura Ashley snow pattern wool sweater for 50 cents in the clothes section, size women's small. I also found a $4.00 linen blouse with faggoting trim on the collar and sleeves and with bone buttons made in Italy. I walk a lot, so I am always looking for accessories. I found an L.L. Bean straw sun hat for $1.50, a wool Stetson hat with leather trim for $1.50, and a gorgeous hand-woven hat made in Australia with leather trim for $1.50.

If you like to read, you can pick up lots of books, magazines, and paperbacks in all flavors. Romance novels, children's books, how-to books, cookbooks, though they tend to be outdated and they are used. You pay one tenth of the original price.

Thrift stores are great for craft items. You'll often find bags of buttons, sewing supplies, bolts of fabrics that are new, and sewing baskets, even sewing machines, irons, and ironing boards.

Any type of basket: White handled baskets hand-painted with roses and leaves. A favorite find for me is a basket made from twisted tree branches.

You can find glassware and silverware that don't necessarily match. Look for real silver, or plate in good condition. Decent buys: Crystal goblet, a set of 4 wine glasses for $4.00. Table cloths, doilies, candlesticks, hand-painted plates, cups and dishes. Also bedspreads, pillows, sheets, baseball caps, purses, tons of totes, bags, handbags.

Occasionally: Wallets, mittens, hand-knitted scarves or shawls, lots of cosmetic bags, any kind you want.

Floral arrangements, vases, a basket filled with gorgeous silk flowers and waxed orchids for $1.50 for the bunch.

Favorite linens: For $5.00, round table topper, fine linen with faggoted edging and white-on-white embroidered flowers.

Luggage: All types of carryons, suitcases, suit bags, flight bags, etc.

Household appliances: hair dryer, curling irons, coffee makers, food processors, washing machines, dryers.

Stuffed animals.

Jewelry, most often costume, but occasionally a selection of gold and silver.

Paintings. You can get originals. I recently started looking for and buying some. A few of my favorites: an Italian villa painting in a walnut frame, signed for $1.00 found at a garage sale; a landscape painting: a golden road in a forest for $3.00, including the ornate gold frame; a bouquet of yellow and orange roses in a gold frame, cost $3.00; and a tiny painting of a bus traveling on a curvy road with poppies and fields in a white antique frame for $4.00.

Thrift Store Shopping in 15 Minutes

Simple rules to follow:

1. Before you go to a thrift store—Decide what you want, know what you are looking for. Bring a list with you, be as specific as needed.

2. Choose a method to shop by: labels, brands, color, size, or style.

Choose one of the above or a combination to shop by. This works really well when you are shopping for clothing purchases, or even household or decorative items.

If you like GAP clothing, and you know it fits you well in a M size—find a rack of clothing and position yourself at one side of the beginning or end of the rack. Look at the rack, then touch the first hanger with your hand. Don't pick it up the item of clothing. Look at the label by pulling the neckline of the garment to see it.

3. Look for it. Can't find it? Ask the store clerk if they've seen it.

4. Look again in a different area of the store where it might be. For example teen sizes or small women's sizes, look in kid's clothing

section. For boots, or oxford-style shoes, look in the men's section. For large women's clothing, look in maternity. For lingerie, look among the evening gowns.

5. Be open to finding something great that you *weren't* looking for.

6. Always ask for a discount if there is something that needs repair.

Here's a sample list from my last thrift store jaunt yesterday:

- Spring wardrobe clothes:—shorts, t-shirts, lightweight pants, swimsuits, casual shoes, low-heeled black shoes for work.

My first stop is the St. Vincent de Paul thrift store. They are having a sale today! Everthing in the store is 25% off except for leather. 25% off at the thrift store is quite nice, not like a Macy's sale!

So the first rack is t-shirts. I don't go through it because they are all regular t-shirts. I like fitted ones. So I go to the rack that has sweaters and blouses. Nothing I like. I go on.

I go to the shoe rack to look for comfy, cute shoes. I see some black leather loafers in my size, barely worn, almost new, square toe. I try them on. They fit! I decide to wear them while I shop. They are Franco Sarto brand. No other shoes looked like they would fit. I move on to look for shorts, casual pants.

There are the two long pants racks. They are divided by color, not size. I flip thorugh the khakis and find a pair of Banana Republic chinos in a size 4. I usually wear a 0 or 2 in their brand. They look small or maybe shrunken. I grab them to try them on. I look through the black pants rack. I find nothing.

I see a swimsuit rack and pull off a couple of bikinis to try on.

There is a rack of shorts. I just look and see if there are any colors or/fabrics that appeal to me. I see some linen shorts in a rich golden color. I pull them off the rack. They are a Ralph Lauren brand label (American Designer). They are petite medium. Maybe . . . they might work. I have to try them on.

I see a rack of women's jackets. I find a nice fitted black ISDA Label in a size 4. I'll try it.

There is a small bin with mostly baseball caps in it. I dig a little. I see a cotton Gap hat, perfect for wearing for walking.

I go to the housewares section where there is a large mirror leaning up against the wall. It is between a shelf filled with glasses and a table with cartons of records on it. Behind me is an old dresser with with houseld items. It's on the side of the store. This is my dressing room. Not for the faint of heart.

Not exactly privacy, but I am prepared. I have leggings on and a long sleeved t-shirt.

I put my pile of stuff , including my purse and the vest I wore into the store, down on the floor in front of the mirror and get started.

I pull the pants on over my leggings. A perfect fit. A little snug over the leggings, so they will likely work and be comfortable.

I try the Gap hat on . . . cute. I'll keep it. I try the shorts on over my leggings. They have a drawstring, so I can pull them in for a tighter fit. One swimsuit was a little worn, I don't even try it. The other swimsuit top was too small. I try the swimsuit top over my t-shirt, over my bra.

Here's what I bought:

- Banana Republic chinos. (Original Price $50.00)

- Ralph Lauren linen shorts (Original Price $ 90.00)

- Gap Cotton Hat (Original Price $20.00)

- Franco Sarto Loafers (Original Price $70.00)

- Bright Blue and Navy Bikini (Original Price $45.00)

My grand total is $12.75
Average price for each item was under $2.55.

Estimated original store price $275.00.
Average price per item $55.00

Total Savings $225.00

On to the next store:

Goodwill is having a sale: all winter clothes, coats, long-sleeved shirts, and sweats are $1. There is madness in the air, clothes flying everywhere. Even though none of the things on sale are on my list, I decide to look for long-sleeved items anyway. I find a sweat shirt and a long sleeved t-shirt to try on. I like to stock up on winter things so I have new things to wear. I go through a few racks of sweaters and come up with nothing. I look for things on my list and go to the shoe rack.

I find a pair of well made leather sandals with an adjustable strap. They are Caressa, Ultima series in my size. I try them on and decide to wear them around the store.

I find a pair of size 2 Old Navy jeans and a pair of jean capris in a size 0. They don't look that small and have lycra in them. I'll try them on. There is a dressing room in this store.

I try on the pants, the size 0 fit perfectly! The size 2s are too small, I can't get them on! You can't always tell by size if something will fit right. Try it on if you can.

As I leave the dressing room, I notice a pair of International Concepts label pants hanging on a rack. One of my favorite brands. They are a size 6. I try them on, they're a little big. But I decide to get them and alter them since I really like the style.

- Leather Sandals by Caressa $4.99 (Original price $65.00)

- Burgundy cotton long-sleeved t-shirt $1.00 (Original price $25.00)

- INC pants (Macy's brand) $5.49 (Original price $70.00)

My grand total is $11.48
Average price for each item was under $3.82

Estimated original store price $160.00
Average price per item $53.00

Total Savings $148.52

So I did good using my list!

I found a pair of shorts, chinos, a pair of sandals, a pair of loafers for work, a pair of slacks, a swimsuit and a t-shirt. No short sleeved t-shirts. Maybe tomorrow. There are lots of thrift stores within 10 minutes of my house, about 20.

On Sunday, where I live there are only two thrift stores that are open, but they are really close to my house so I go there.

One is the Goodwill and the other is the St. Vincent de Paul. (Read the story about him, he was a really cool guy, the original social services worker for the poor. There is even a black and white film about him that I rented through the public library for free.)

The Goodwill store is so popular in my neighborhood that it is now open 7 days a week from 10 am to 9 pm! Whenever I have a thrift store attack, I can go there!

I admit it, I am addicted to thrift stores and bargain hunting. It is fun and relaxing.

There Is No Dressing Room in the Store, What Do I Do?

At some thrift stores there is no dressing room. Most of the time the clothes will be cheaper for this reason. What do you do? Jackets, coats, sweaters, shirts, and vests can be tried on over a t-shirt, or thin sweater. Skirts and dresses you can try on over your clothes. Pants are the hardest to try on, but I try them on over pants, or leggings.

Wear your leggings, tightest pants or shorts, or workout clothes.

If the clothes are comfortable and fit snug—they are probably just the right fit. The stores that do have tags attached will sometimes allow you to return them as long as the tag is still there. Always try things on, even over your clothes!

You can measure waist and length with a tape measure, or simply buy brands you know. You can also buy it by size or appearance.

A friend just told me about a Goodwill that has clothing for $1.00 and they have a dressing room. I am ready to go. She told me she picked up a pair of Gap khakis and Banana Republic khakis. And a pair of slacks for work. You can't beat that!

Knowing about one item is your best resource in finding treasures at you local thrift shop. You may not care about clothes, but if you love dishes or furniture, those are good things to start with. If you know tea cups or dolls and recognize the quality of something and its worth, start there.

Take any department store. You decide you need a pair of jeans. What kind of jeans are you looking for? To wear around the house, to work in the yard, or to wear on a date with someone you want to impress? If you're at the department store you can pick up the cheapest pair, and go to the surplus store to get working in the yard jeans.

I've gone through stages of things I buy at thrift stores. When I started a job last year doing freelance makeup, I had to wear all black. Well, going out and buying a whole new black wardrobe was going to be a large investment. So every time I go to the thrift store, I look for clothing that's black, then I look for my size, and fabric. I try it on and if I like it I buy it. I now have a very complete black wardrobe that includes scarves, shoes, belts, jewelry, t-shirts, blouses, jackets, skirts, sweaters, and pants. All these items are of very high quality.

Determining Value

One easy way to find the value of things to go to department stores, or any kind of quality store to see how much things cost. Go to all different types of stores, go to exclusive department stores, specialty shops, and boutiques.

You can do this online, or with catalogues, too. Look at the best items, not how much you can afford.

PBS's Antiques Road Show is a great primer for getting you going and understanding the difference between value and worth. It does not matter how much you pay for something, or where you bought it. It is what it is to you, or to someone else. In any case, you should know its value if you decide to sell it. I enjoy watching the Antiques Road show for that very reason. People on the show are always showing up with something they found which was either given to them, or they paid a pittance for at a garage sale, flea market, or thrift store.

A man on the show had an Indian blanket his parents had given him: a plain large black and off-white wool blanket. It turned out to be worth $350,000.00 to $500,000.00, possibly more. Everyone was gasping for air, including me.

Another man had a pretty golden vase shaped like a shell that he had hidden on a closet shelf. It was a Lalique vase worth thousands. Another man bought a table from a friend for $600.00. The show valued it at $100,000.00.

I haven't had that much good fortune yet. But I enjoy collecting pretty things for my home such as

- a bubble glass amber colored vase for I got for $3.00

- a bunch of silk flowers: poppies, orchids and white wax orchids with green foilage for $1.50 (enough for three vases full of bouquets!), and a large wicker planter for $3.00

Other recent purchases:
- a brand new matching taupe and beige couch and ottoman for $200.00

- an original painting of yellow and orange vases with matching frame for $3.00

- a lovely original landscape painting with frame for $3.00

- 2 large rectangular oak mirrors from a dresser (which I painted gold), $40.00 for the pair.

- a compact washer/dryer for $100.00 that I bought from a neighbor moving out

The same concept applies. Buy quality, reject poor quality regardless of the price, or where you buy it. I have not gone out looking for Indian blankets or Lalique vases. Collectors do. My point is that you can find value everywhere. You just have to educate yourself regarding its true worth. Discover the quality you can buy.

I had a male friend who bought shirts by the dozen at the thrift store. I was cheaper to buy them, and wear one a day. He could take them into a cleaner and has a whole new set.

I confine myself mostly to clothing, but also have bought furniture, baskets, and

- a fax machine which cost $50.00 at a garage sale

- $50.00 art deco chest, matching Italian glass top table and black lacquer chairs for $350.00

- scrolled iron wine racks for $3.00

- 4 woven round place mats for $1.00

- a brand new large basket for $3.99.

What do you need to know to shop confidently at any store or thrift store? You must to know what you are looking for. Determine if it works for you. Check it out, to make sure it is a quality item and if the item is worth being fixed, repaired, or altered, etc.? Are you going to do it, or someone else?

Tips for Shopping for Quality

Look for pure natural fabrics such as wool, cotton, silk, rayon, and blends are good with less than 50% polyester and nylon.

Linings on clothing are most often found on better quality clothing. If you found clothing with a silk lining, you have a real find. Hand rolled or stitched linings are a rarity, except in the best clothing. How do you tell the difference? Most lining fabrics are rayon/acetate, a thin. crispy taffeta-like fabric. The better rayon/acetate linings are thicker, heavier, and more satin like, softer in feel.

The feel of wool can be scratchy, stiff, thick, and rough, or it can be soft, finely woven, and well-draped. I like to touch fabrics to see how they feel. All better fabrics drape and hang on the body better, which give them that quality look. They hold their colors better, stay true longer. I like soft fabrics, they are easier to wear, but generally take more care in cleaning, they have to be hand washed or dry cleaned.

Carefully check out skirts, linings, hems (for straightness and evenness.

Look for buttons: horn, leather shell, crystal, and bone.

Look for quality labels that you know or are familiar with: Gap, Ann Taylor, Banana Republic, Liz Claiborne.

On coats, check the linings. Look for cashmere, alpaca.

Slacks and trousers: look for pockets or pants with linings. Linings are a sign of quality.

Unhemmed pants or skirts means they are new.

On shirts, frayed edges on collars or cuffs are not a good sign.

In blouses, especially silk, look for evenness of the dye color. Look for rolled edges.

Scarves in silk, wool, cashmere, and mohair.

Jeans, check out the evenness of stitching, flat with no puckers.

These concepts are available to you anywhere you may shop. Quality endures, fashion fades. Trends come and go. Function and usefulness are trademarks of quality and classic styling.

How To Tell Quality Shoes Quickly

Look at leather soles, lining, the bottom of the shoes. The best are made in Italy or Spain with a stamp on the bottom, and the soles are usually thicker. The leather is usually softer. I look for all leather. The most I have ever paid for a pair of shoes has been $10.00. I found 3 pairs of Cole-Haans: hand stitched loafers in navy, tan, and bone. These retail from $150.00 and up, per pair. Brand new and never worn! Was I happy that day, and I wear a narrow size!

Shoes are one of the best buys for me. I have a narrow foot, but still wear orthotics. I have even gone to Nordstrom, and could not find a pair of shoes that fit me that I liked. Just this week I found a 8N dressy oxford Anne Klein for $10.00 in perfect condition. That made my year for shoes!

Accessories

Accessories are one of the best buys at a thrift store. If you like baseball caps, there is always a tub full. This winter was so cold I decided that I needed and wanted more berets and hats. So I decided to pick up more, to add to my collection. It has been colder than usual in California.

- Mauve angora/acrylic knitted beret for $3.00

- Macy's Marchiones 100% wool cream knitted cap

- Canadian wool knitted purple, size small, brim cap (last year's cost $4.00.)

- Betmar taupe trimmed soft wool hat for $3.00

- Alpaca-trimmed knit hat with tri-color band, off-white, for $3.00

- Italian bubble knit, wool blend brim hat with brown velvet trim.

- Black velvet brim soft hat with red black green roses.

- Black velvet satin lined beret with covered buttons for $1.50

- Two flat knit cotton berets, royal blue, and orange, brand new with tags attached for $4.00 each

- GAP virgin wool classic beret for $2.00

Other great accessories to look for are scarves, purses, and sunglasses. I buy sunglasses by the dozens at thrift stores, because I am always losing them, and breaking them. I buy them for 50 cents to $5.00. I always have a spare.

I like vintage scarves, usually silk or rayon that look handpainted. In mufflers, I bought mohair wool pink fringed scarf, made in Scotland with a Harrod's label for $3.00. An angora/cashmere shawl made in Italy in pale green for $4.00. A Bennetton scarf in a deep green, in soft ribbed wool. In London, I bought a curly boa scarf in brilliant velvet for 2 pounds.

Leather belts are an expensive accessory anywhere except at the thrift store.

If you want the latest look, If you want stylish pants that fit well and look good with a certain pair of boots—you will probably going to have to pay a good price for them. I generally do not buy jeans at the thrift store because I like the hipper trendier looks, which are much harder to find at a thrift store. You can find them, but they may take a little longer to find. If you want every day wearable jeans, Levi's, wranglers, carpenter pants, army pants, get them at the thrift store for $1.00 to $10.00. For trendier jeans styles, I buy them at outlets, large department stores, discount stores, and wait for sales.

The last pair of jeans I bought at Nordstroms in December were $77.00 jeans at half-off, plus a 20% discount. I worked there over the holidays. This was very pricey for me, but I wear them all the time. So, I am getting my money's worth out of these jeans.

Things to Check Before You Buy

Say you find a Brooks Brothers cashmere sweater for $3.00. You will need to look for obvious wear and tear, holes, buttons missing, and stains. Look at the necklines and elbows for wear or thinning of fabric. Hold the garment up to the light. Test the seams on each side, on the neck and shoulders.

For sweaters: remember that thinner knits are

harder to repair, but seams can usually be repaired. Bulkier sweaters also can be repaired, as long as the hole is not too large. You can take it to the cleaners, most do alterations, or get a recommendation from a friend. If it's thinning anywhere I would not buy it, it's too expensive to repair.

Anything that is tailored can be taken up, or in—larger is better, but not too large, not more than 2 sizes bigger than you usually wear. Jackets can be fitted. Shoulder pads can be put in, or taken out, and buttons changed. Hems can be shortened, or lengthened, check out the hem to make sure there is enough material. Linings can be replaced if torn, or stained. I would not recommend this unless it is something that you really like a lot, or are going to wear a lot. It can be costly. Pants can be taken in at the waist and fitted through the thighs. You could buy a quality pair of jeans at the thrift store, and have them custom fitted for $30.00 to $40.00. Still cheaper and much more flattering.

Shopping: Consignment Stores vs. Thrift Stores

You can see how it works. I have two consignment stores that I regularly consign to. One is Labels—a designer consignment store. They sell European and designer clothing. For example, a Chanel suit's original retail price was $2,000.00. In the consignment store, it is selling for $600.00. They also carry Gap, Banana Republic, and vintage items. I usually have an average of $50.00 credit. Since I like "new" clothes so much, I occasionally buy more pricey, or hard to find items.

I took a couple of friends shopping at Labels. They were both looking for evening attire for a dressy event coming up.

Clarice found a caftan for at home entertaining for $20.00, and found an evening bag for $15.00. She put a luxurious coat to wear out in the evening on hold. Jacque found a basic black velvet dress with ribbon trim, and an everyday Talbot tan leather handbag for $15.00. I found a cinnamon brown cashmere turtleneck body suit from Donna Karan, and it was selling for $66.00—but, I had credit in the store! It cost me $23.00. That was a luxurious find and some super good buys.

Yesterday it was cold and rainy in California, 35 degrees, and I decided I needed a coat. In January coats are usually priced for clearance, so I could expect to get a good buy! A friend told me she bought a $300.00 coat for 75% off at Macy's. It costs $75.00. I decided to go to the thrift stores first. I found a brand-new bright red knee-length rain coat, a London Fog, for $17.00. I also found a wool angora cashmere-blend carcoat from Ann Taylor for $4.00 that was missing one button.

I went to the fabric store and bought a selection of buttons for $2.49, found one to match and sewed it on. It matches.

Another trick I have learned is to buy damaged and worn out garments—just for the buttons. You can pick up a beat-up garment for $1.00, and get $10.00 worth of buttons. Look for decorative shell, horn, wood, carved brass, and leather buttons on jackets. Get a whole matching set.

For instance, I found a classic wrap knee-length camelhair coat for $10.00. It fit, but it was a little too snug to be comfortable, so I turned it down. I could go back and get it and put it on consignment, but it is a risk.

Sales at Thrift Stores?! Markdowns at Consignment Stores?!

Do not forget that when a thrift store gets overloaded with clothes, books, furniture, etc., they have a sale anywhere from 20% to 50% off already low prices. Some thrift stores overprice on certain items. I can not say why—other than the person managing the store thinks of the worth of those items more than they are. Of course the opposite can happen too! That is how you can find a cashmere sweater for $3.00.

One of my favorite thrift stores has a standard price for everything. For example: records are $1.00; shoes' $3.00; boots are $5.00; skirts' $3.00; pants' $3.00; sweaters' $3.00, suites' $10.00 and blouses are $2.00. So, an acrylic sweater from K-Mart is the same price as a cashmere sweater from Macy's. Or a silk blouse from Nordstroms is the same price as a polyester blouse from Sears.

There are more thrift stores, and they all compete with each other. Thrift stores have all kinds of incentives and discounts.

1. A clearance rack with 50% off the original price.

2. Every Saturday their clothes are 50% off, and they have special sales events for holidays too.

3. Another store has 20% off for Senior discounts daily.

4. A senior discount of 50% is offered every Tuesday.

5. Merchandise is marked down by 50% by a due date specified on the tag.

6. A $1.00 (one dollar) rack in the back of the store.

7. A card that you stamp for every $10.00 you spends. When you have spent $100.00, over a period of a year, you get $10.00 off your next purchase.

8. Sometimes there are even free things given away in front of the store or in the store.

   For example: bread, pastries, furniture, books, magazines, toiletries, hangers, boxes, clothing, dishes, etc.

9. Hourly specials.

10. All sweaters are 50% off today.

11. Bag days. $2.00 to $10.00 to fill a bag with anything. I actually found a gorgeous wool coat, plus other items that day for $2.00 per bag.

Shopping Cheap Elsewhere

Flea markets—People usually have stalls set up according to the type of things they are selling. Sunglasses, clothing, furniture, toys, cosmetics, collectibles. It is like a giant garage sale. If you really don't mind haggling, go there. You can find good deals but have to know your merchandise well. Some things are way overpriced.

Flea markets in Europe are the place to go. Paris flea markets are fun, and you can get anything there. London Charity Shops—Forget them, we have the best thrift stores in America.

Garage Sales—Best for furniture, but you have to get there early for the best selection. Or call the day before to see what they have. Wait until the end of the day and get the best deals on whatever is left. Garage sales are great for kids clothing and accessories. Set aside at least half a day or a whole day to do this.

Outlets—If you want the latest trends shop the outlets. But beware, you can get damaged or irregular merchandise. Prices can be like department store sale prices.

Department Store Sales—You *can* get good buys. Get there early, pre-shop, put on hold. Develop relationships with salespeople for the best service and tips.

Rummage sales, Tag sales—These are usually more organized with articles priced to sell. You can find great things, but why wait for your favorite organization to have one, go to a thrift store!

Dollar Stores—You can get top quality new merchandise, everything from food, shoes, clothing for women and children, household items, linens, toys, cleaning supplies, costume jewelry, party supplies, craft supplies, trinkets and more.

Selling/Consigning Your Stuff

If you want to make money off your stuff:

Look under
Consignment stores.
Clothing—men, women and kids.
Household—trinket, dishes and collectibles.
Furniture—stores, paintings, chairs, tables, lamps.
flea markets—sell it yourself.
Garage sales—sell it yourself.
Bay area swap parties.
Save stuff for a neighbor,
Give kids' clothes to a friend, including baby items.

Some stores will buy outright and pay cash on the spot for certain things.
Jewelry, fine and costume:
Pawn shops.
Clothing consignment stores.
Vintage stores.
Jewelry stores.

Private parties—through classified ads.
Furs—Coats.

Check with consignment stores, before going in.
Books.
Thrift stores.
Used book stores.
Office Equipment.
Donate to charities and non-profit organizations.

Recycle
Preserving our resouces, and energy—how much energy went into making that piece of clothing? Quite a bit—I know.

What to do with clothing?
Old, stained clothes, T-shirts and towels can be cut up and used as cleaning/wash rags.
Socks make great polishing cloths for furniture and shoes.
Old sundresses can be used as nightgowns.
An old sweater becomes a robe.
Old sweats make great cold night pajamas.
Long johns make good pajamas
Berets become head warmers at night.
Coats become blankets for extra warmth.
Jeans become cut-offs or a purse.
Cotton or silk shirts become pajamas or loungewear.
Lightweight Cotton, rayon or silk pants become pajamas or lounge wear or evening wear.

T-shirts may become long underwear.

Thick socks can be used as slippers.

Save fancy buttons from an old garment and sew or put on to another garment.

Shawls can be used as a table cloth, window covering, draped on chairs or sofas.

Scarves/ribbon can be used for tying gifts or tying back curtains or wrapped around a pillow or a gift planter.

Household Items can be used for:

Rugs become wall hangings.

Large straw purses can become paper holders and wastebaskets and planters.

Old trunks can be used as coffee tables, storage, plant stand.

A kitchen table can become a computer desk or work table.

Small tables, stools or chairs can be used as end tables, to hold plants or objets d'art.

Plates (chipped) mugs, bowls can become planters.

Old dresser can be a side board.

A free standing shelf can become a shoe holder.

Laundry baskets can hold purses and stored fabrics.

An incense holder can become a flower holder.

Wrapping paper becomes liners for drawers or used for crafts.

Old notebooks become journals, or scratch pads.

Baskets can be used as fruit bowls, napkin holders, bread holders, a snack tray, a magazine holder, wastebasket or paper holder.

Mugs become pencil holders, planters, even key holders or paper clip holders, rubber bands.

Use mirrors from bureaus as decorative objects all over the house.

Linens, doilies, napkins, and tablecloths can be used for craft projects as curtains, wall hangings or framed.

Frame favorite music, book covers or prints, magazine photos.

What you can do with things:

Use mirrors from bureaus all over the house. Look for vintage lines, doilies, napkins, and tablecloths. They can be bleached and starched. They last forever.

Many times you will find a framed print with no glass. You can get that replaced. You can buy framed prints, as well. You can buy the print and change the frame too, or vice versa. It is a good place to buy frames.

Obviously, not all stores carry all things. I've seen collectors, and shoppers come in and buy everything the store may have from stuffed animals, chairs, glasses, vases, coats, and hats, etc.

Hand lotions, creams: use as hair styling gel, defrizzers.

Shampoos: clear or colored use for hand washables.

Touch up costume jewelry and buttons with nail polish.

Use mascara: to thicken up your eye brows or cover gray hair on a mustache or sideburns

Tool boxes: large and small, make great make-up kits craft/sewing supplies.

Baby-wipes: use for quick face cleaning, removing spots on clothes, floors anywhere and for freshening up.

Eye shadows: wet them and use as an eye-liner or for eyebrows.

Care For, Restore, and Repair Your Treasures!

I keep clothes and accessories for years, so far, up to 20 years, that I still use! First of all, they are quality and quality lasts, no matter how much you paid for or where you bought it.

If I bought a quality pair of shoes for a good price and they need a small repair, it is worth it to take it to get fixed. Shoes can resoled, dyed, or reheeled at a good shoe repair shop. Purses can be repaired, zippers replaced, purse handles changed. Belts can be shortened, holes added, buckles and snaps replaced. I have had boots that last me for years. I take them in every year to have them resoled and reheeled. Straps can be replaced, insoles put in or taken out, or lining added to shoes. Stretching shoes is not a reliable practice.

The first thing I do when I buy something from a thrift store is air it out and put it on a hanger.

Sweaters of cashmere, wool, and wool blends, wash by hand in cool water, dry overnight, flat on a towel and reshape.

Take all suits and jackets, tailored skirts and blouses and silk items to the cleaners.

Jeans, denim, cotton T-shirts, sweatshirts, wash in cold water and cool dryer.

Leather items such as shoes, purses, wallets and luggage, clean with a leather cleaner, polish and wax and/or use leather balm as often as needed to keep it new looking.

I generally don't buy suede, unless it is in mint condition.

If something is missing buttons and can be easily replaced, especially on a coat, the repair may be worth it. Do take into account the cost of cleaning and alterations, but it will still be generally less than half the cost of a new coat.

Things I Like to Collect at Thrift Stores

Purses. I have a thing for small purses, vintage, or otherwise. Here's a list of the purses that I have found, gathered, and collected in my own private treasure chest. One favorite is a brown leather (possibly alligator) box purse with a brass clasp suit case style, for only $3.99 that is worth between $100.00 to $800.00. A vintage 30s Forde black cord bag with brass clasp, bought for $5.00, worth $40.00. A Majestic (brand) plexiglass bucket evening bag with gold lace and plated hardware cost me $5.00, and is worth $200.00 to $300.00. Another is a 50s clear-cut plastic inset with rhinestones clutch bag. A small Coach tan leather bag cost $3.00. Black leather alligator-embossed tiny bag with silver trim. An Esprit black velvet mini-bag, and a black 50s leather rolled bag with double handles.

I like certain vintage things that are wearable and classic, such as handbags, jackets, coats, skirts, some dresses. and blouses. I tend to mix eras of clothes for a unique classic look. For New Year's I wore a satin stretch J. Crew slack with a 50s vintage beaded cream sweater and a black sequined beret. It's a very timeless, simple, fun, sparkly look.

Getting Rid of Stuff? Who To Give It To

Where to go? Look in the yellow pages under the header thrift stores, charity shops, secondhand stores.

If you want to donate to a favorite charity, call them and ask them if they have a thrift store, or if they will take quality things to use at auction. You can receive a tax deduction from items such as crystal candlesticks to services to cars. Instead of going to the dump or trash, haul it to the thrift store as long as it is good enough to resell, usable or workable. Film and theater people and non-profits look there for often for worn looking clothing, furniture, etc. for their productions.

Nonprofit organizations
Teen centers
Shelters for battered women
Career closets
Homeless families
Other countries
Christmas holiday programs for the poor

All of these organizations can use quality items. Please check to find out what they need. Some only accept new merchandise. But you can usually receive a tax deductible donation.

Conclusion

The shopping techniques I have outlined in *90% OFF—Every Day!* can be applied anywhere you shop. These skills will help you shop in outlets, department store sales, warehouses, anywhere. Your shopping experiences will be more efficient, focused and with better results.

I am obviously quite partial to shopping at thrift stores. There is nowhere else you can find such a wide variety of merchandise from all over the country, the world and different eras all in one place. It is cheap, fun, entertaining and educational. Your shopping experience can be as practical or as extravagant as you make it to be, depending on what you find or look for.

Shopping will even raise your endorphin levels! An elderly woman I met while doing some informal research said that a health organization reccomended shopping as a positive activity because of this. She couldn't afford to, so she started going to thrift stores. It has become an important activitiy for her health and well-being as well as her pocketbook.

Shopping at thrift stores can help you save loads of money by reducing your expenses in what you choose to purchase there. Think of all the savings you could make on furniture, collectibles, antiques, baby, children's, teen's, men's and women's clothing, shoes, coats, belts, purses, hats, books, sporting goods, household items, appliances, and whatever else you could come across.

Shopping at thrift stores helps to preserve our resources and provides money to help needy individuals, charities, valuable communiy programs and organizations. We live in a country that is abundantly blessed with material goods. Most of us have too much and have to rent storage space to hold it. If you are not using it, please give it away so someone else can use it. So before you throw anything out, please drop it off—donate it to the thrift store. Remember you can even get a tax deduction for getting rid of what you don't need.

As the saying goes, one person's junk is another person's treasure. Shopping at thrift stores is a real treasure hunt anyone can afford. Great shopping adventures to you!

Diana Tenes
October, 2002

Filmography for Diana Tenes from IMDB.com Internet Movie Database

Actress (8 titles)
2009 The Filmmaker Couch Candice
2009 Everything Strange and NewManny's Wife
2009 Darker Every Day Make-Up Artist
2009 I (Almost) Got Away with It(TV series) Maria
2006 Stupid CupidJean
2006 The Home Front (short)
2001 I, Detective (TV series) X-wife who hires a hitman
1999 Change Is Hard (TV short) Shame Mother

Make-Up Department (6 titles)
2009 The Filmmaker (makeup artist)
2010 Titans of Yoga (documentary) (makeup artist)
2006 Soledad Is Gone Forever (short) (key makeup artist)
2005 After Life (short) (key makeup artist)
2005 Widow Maker (short) (makeup artist)
2003 Simply Wine with Andrea Immer (TV series) (key makeup)

Costume Designer (2 titles)
2006 Fat Rose and Squeaky
2004 Kwoon (video)
Costume and Wardrobe Department (1 title)
2009 The Filmmaker (costumer)

Diana's Selected Celebrity Clientele:for Make-up:
Charlene Tilton: Actress " Lucy Ewing" on Dallas TV series Malou Nubla:
Producer/Media Personality Two time Emmy Award Winner Mike Rowe: Media
Personality/Host of "Dirty Jobs" on Discovery Channel Susan Hammer: Mayor
San Jose Lilias Folan: "The First lady of Yoga" "Lilias Yoga and You" on
PBS Dr. Dean Ornish: Physician consultant to President Clinton Dharma
Mittra: Master Yoga Chart of 1,000 postures Sharon Gannon and David Life:
Founders of Jivamukti Yoga

Diana's Selected Celebrity Clientele for Wardrobe:
Julie Brown: Actress/comedian/producer
Lea de Laria: Broadway singer/comedian/actress Louise Fletcher:
Actress/Academy Award winner as Nurse Ratchett Cicely Tyson: Actress/Emmy
Award winner, Academy Award nominee

www.ingramcontent.com/pod-product-compliance
Lightning Source LLC
Chambersburg PA
CBHW071432040426
42445CB00012BA/1352